SNOWLINE AND OTHER DISTANCES

SNOWLINE AND OTHER DISTANCES

THOMAS FASANO

Coyote Canyon Press
Claremont, California

Copyright © 2025 by Thomas Fasano

All rights reserved.

No part of this publication may be reproduced, distributed, or transmitted in any form or by any means, including photocopying, recording, or other electronic or mechanical methods, without the prior written permission of the author, except in the case of brief quotations embodied in critical reviews and certain other noncommercial uses permitted by copyright law.

First Edition

Table of Contents

Temporal Fray 1
Twilight's Paradox 2
Cycles of the Merciless 3
Reclaimed Whispers 4
Seasonal Palimpsest 5
Refractive Confluence 6
Crevice Light 7
Decay Clarity 8
Leafscript 9
Linguistic Botany 10
Winter's Geometry 11
Cycles of Stir 12
Gorge Light 13
Winter's Soliloquy 14
Echoes of the Mundane 15
Threshold Echoes 16
Subtracting Daylight 17
Temporal Mingle 18
Choreographic Courses 19
Temporal Contours 20
Frost's Script 21
Eternal Tangles 22
Thresholds of Dawn 23
Chiaroscuro Whispers 24
Temporal Mimes 25
Frost Whispers 26
Granite Whispers 27
Seasons of Embrace 28
Domestic Orbits 29
Winter's Murmur 30
Marsh Mithridatism 31
Thaw's Dance 32
Incremental Thaw 33
"Frost and Flame" 34
Bridge of Whispers 35
Cityscape Mornings 36
Echo's Symphony 37

Temporal Mirroring	38
Internal Marketplace	39
Scatter of Resilience	40
Temporal Echoes	41
Mechanics of Indifference	42
Whispers of Growth	43
Winter's Mind	44
Winter's Palimpsest	45
Thawing Transactions	46
Chill Sublime	47
Winter's Dialogue	48
Winter's Ballet	49
Erosion's Tongue	50
Thaw's Alchemy	51
Seasonal Cadence	52
Seasonal Constructs	53
Thaw's Philosophy	54
Whispers of Shape	55
Horizon Echoes	56
Misty Interlude	57
Season's Thaw	58
Thresholds of Unrest	59
Temporal Whispers	60
Transient Thaws	61
Existence Erased	62
Thresholds of Thought	63
Seasonal Scrolls	64
Season's Echo	65
Frost Schemes	66
Interplay of Warmth and Whims	67
Twilight Sculptures	68
Thaw's Murmur	69
Transient Skies	70
Ripple Narratives	71
Unscripted Gracing	72
Temporal Stillness	73
Whispered Dusk	74

Winter's Whispers	75
Winter's Symphony	76
Entropy and Echo	77
Surface Depths	78
Endless Cycle	79
Philosophy in Motion	80
Fracture Symmetry	81
Web of Unself	82
Convergent Divergence	83
Echoes and Horizons	84
Breath of the Void	85
Stone to Bone	86
Cosmic Necessity	87
Frost's Retreat	88
White Whispers	89
Celestial Thread	90
Canvas of Truth	91
Memory's Current	92
Edge Resolves	93
Brooksong Essence	94
Endurance Paradox	95
Seasonal Self	96
Temporal Waltz	97

Temporal Fray

Leaves whisper down: a slow descent
as time itself bends, arches, spent,
the pheasant springs—the brush: its cleft—
moments seize us, lost, bereft.
    Skinned branches swipe, the wind's harsh scrip,
    black crows circle, their cries encrypt.

Draped in mist, the world softens,
  shadows blend with fading suns;
Pharmacy aisles—halos of pills,
pick up comfort, soothe the chills.
A poem spills: ink flows, blooms,
words to hold as silence looms.

Life's fabric worn, threads thin, pull apart,
each stitch a day, each tear a heart.
    Yet in this soft, relentless fray,
truths unveiled in stark display—
Aging's quiet symphony plays,
as night enfolds our numbered days.

Twilight's Paradox

Beneath the twilight's dwindling eye:
whispers curl like leaves in wind,
    murmuring to the silenced ones
whose shadows flicker on the verge
of gold leaf and the reddened dusk:
each hue a note in nature's score.

  Thus, the living hold the cup—
brimmed with dregs of memories—
drinking to stillness, heart's restraint
where silence wraps its gentle shroud.
  Mourners lace their grief with gold:
the lavish pain of holding on.

But serene are those who rest,
beyond the reach of weeping's echo:
unheld by joy, untouched by sorrow—
a bitter peace in this soft paradox.
Free from the cycle's savage tooth
  that gnaws at those who yet remain.

Cycles of the Merciless

In the swamp's deep folds, decay festers:
    buzzards circle, their shadows crisping
    the ground: the sun, a relentless preacher,
    turns maggots into shimmering rivers.
    Amidst the murk, life pulses, relentless
as a jaguar's gaze: stilled yet burning,

sharp as the viper's poised silence,
waiting, knowing death's impartial dance.
  They watch as seasons strip the trees bare,
  birds skim tops, seldom nesting, restless:
everything blown away, dust to air:
here, life cycles with merciless flair.

Change whispers through reeds, a subtle thief,
    stealing greens, leaving gold-rust splotches,
    the air a loose stitch unraveling, light
    slanting toward colder angles. Each leaf
a tattered script of wind-worn breath—
raccoons scavenge, indifferent, unwound.

Reclaimed Whispers

Amidst the clutter we discard, nature
finds a way: a jay dips, its cobalt wings
clash with the grey of broken things,
    naming each discarded shard
  a perch, a treasure, undimmed by our disdain:
a mosaic of the tossed-aside, reformed.

Leaves, a flutter above the commerce of neglect,
    rustle a softer script: here is life,
unpriced, thriving within the scatter,
where sunlight catches the jagged edge
of glass, turning trash into prisms,
casting rainbows on the doubts of value.

Branches sway, a slow dance of resilience,
bending, not breaking, under the weight
of our dismissals: each leaf whispers
a defiance, a creed of inherent worth,
beyond the ugliness we assign—
wind-swept, they stand, rooted yet reaching.

Seasonal Palimpsest

    Leaves whisper down: life's gentle decay,
      Autumn cloaks my shoulders with cool air,
    Reeds bow under weight of geese, arrayed
In V's sharp as life's sudden despair:
Cedarberries darken, blood-rich hue,
A sign of seasons shifting anew.

Sky, a canvas rinsed by recent rain,
    Holds layers of gray and forgotten blue,
    Each drop a memory, a stain,
Merging past's purity with what's true:
The ground softens, embraces each fall,
    Leaves mixing with earth, heeding the call.

    In this cycle, where ends brush beginnings,
Roots delve deep in quiet strength, unseen:
My hands trace lines, life's map thinning,
While hi-flo glyphs etch between.
Yet in decline, a vibrant thread—
    Life's fabric woven, unwoven, then spread.

Refractive Confluence

Winds shift the course of the brook: its surge
meets the cold, clear glass of thought, refracts:
where edges soften, merge, the water chants
its ancient runes, a glossary of murk
and sparkle: how the stream ribs the mud,
cradling droplets, crafting history.

Tall reeds listen: the wind's philosophy,
dialogues scripted in sediment scrawl:
the mockingbird mimics the rush, the fall,
    each call a question marked by urgency.
Waters twist, insisting: look deeper, see
between the lines where shadows speak truth.

    Edges where water and glass confront each truth:
  a prism, bending light to expose rifts
in perception: where clarity shifts,
creating spectra out of the clear blue.
  Nature's discourse—brooks burbling, a view
unasked, telling in its persistent flow.

Crevice Light

In this slice of earth the land cleaves:
neat fissures split the soil, logic lost;
trees crack mid-growth, limbs split into air,
and human trails dissolve into the mist;
    each step: a gamble on whether the ground
will hold or fold beneath a trembling foot.

Neck wires strain against a sudden gap:
hair tie snaps, freedom in the fracture.
   The sorghum broomcane sweeps over dust
     and rock, paused by jarring intervals
that nature grids in unseen patterns,
binds us by the chance of crossing.

Yet in these breaches blooms the wild fern:
a testament to crevice-dwelling light,
and beneath the chasm's threatening yawn,
a rivulet whispers, persists, carves a path
  through hushed scenes of ruptured terrain—
continues threading life's fragile seam.

Decay Clarity

Leaves decay in quiet whispers,
    wet shadows underfoot: they block,
preserve the barren darkness,
   a mat where nothing dares to grow:
the sharp scent of walnut, bitter,
    spreads its sterile creed.

Twisted branches write in sky-scripts,
broken sentences of life and interruption,
each leaf a word, fallen, unresolved:
   how the clarity of decay obscures,
    yet reveals: tangled roots grasping,
searching for a hold in shifting soil.

This landscape, dense with stasis, breathes
  a quiet frustration: choked potential,
where thoughts, like undergrowth, tangle
  unsprouted, their whispers lost in wind,
    while solitude deepens, echoing
      the ungraspable heart of existence.

Leafscript

Leaves swirl at the stone steps: a storm
of greens spurned by the brisk talk of wind,
dancing to the hum of the ancient facade,
   where knowledge is stored, bound neatly in skin.
Yet, outside, life twirls—a vivid disarray
   scripted by gusts that scorn the straight line.

Starlings weave through the air: a script
penned in the moment's pulse, snapping berries
from the ivy's cold, clingy fingers.
   Their wings beat—soft thrums—against the hush
of books, where dust layers the unturned page,
a slow sedimentation unseen by the eye.

The breeze does not read; it scatters
   ephemera across the asphalt's blank slate,
each leaf laid, then lifted: a lesson
in temporary truths that, unlike stone,
will shift, degrade, yet in that change,
feed new cycles that books alone cannot teach.

Linguistic Botany

Beneath our feet, the roots twist: words,
like threads, weave through dark soils of mind,
   melding with minerals: truths obscured
by the tangled braid of roots confined.
We speak, and branches stir: the power
of language: both shield and spear.

    Yet, in this synthetic bloom, the flower
emerges not from sun, but sheer
force of phrase, petal by stanza grown,
each syllable a seed from which realities
   spring, misted by the breath, alone,
that speaks them into form, breeds dualities.

   The garden here is mind-made: fertile, lush,
an echo of the wild, yet calm, hush.
In this crafted landscape, where clarity
   seems as mutable as cloud-cover,
a sudden sunbreak splits: rarity,
revealing how much words can alter.

Winter's Geometry

Bare branches hold the sky: light sieves
   through willow bones, reaching for evergreens that
never sleep, anchored in frost's grip,
a contrast: life pulsing under the bark, waiting
     for the thaw, while snow ensnares root and creek
in its crystal lattice, winter's strict geometry.

Footprints weave stories in the white: a mouse's
scant trace beside the deeper press of a deer,
life scaled in juxtaposition, fleeting and deep,
   the snow remembers each step, till sun
      and wind revise the text, ephemeral as breath
     on glass: the silence echoes with continuance.

How a father's words linger, etching frost on windows,
    while his hands, long stilled, mimic branches
against the light: teachings that hold against
     the cold. Spry traces of pheasant stitch through
the drifts, life asserting amidst the still,
     each motion a testament to the enduring pulse.

Cycles of Stir

Wind stirs the wheat field's golden waves:
each stalk a slender thought, engaging
in the dance of light and shadow,
  photons cascading down like rain.
Gravity, that old tug on the seed's
deep rest: it rouses, splits,

   twists upward through loam, reaching,
each moment a stretch against entropy.
   Tiny roots, a network, silent yet shouting.
The sun arcs; photons convert:
leaves revel in the chemistry of living,
breathing out what we breathe in,

a looping exchange, seamless and endless.
   Night descends, cool drapes pulling
across the stage of day. Stars pierce the dark,
mirroring our neurons' spark.
   Even in sleep, life hums within cells,
  murmurs of mitochondria, whispers.

Gorge Light

Across the gash of gorge, light slips:
a thread thrown through the dark's mass,
　splaying its fingers on the rocks
　　and shadows that dance like fears
in minds cornered by doubt's edge.
　　It scatters wide, this fragile clarity.

　Yet, it navigates: each dip and rise
mapped in pulses of persistent glow,
bouncing on the cavities that speak
　of deeper, unseen worlds below.
　　The resilience of its path
in grapy glass, captured, fleeting.

　Through the veil of night, it persists,
　　a testament to the obstinate pulse
　　of understanding, perennially reborn
from the cocoon of confusion.
　　Its journey—a parable woven
from the loom of perpetual return.

Winter's Soliloquy

    Snow layers down with a quiet insistence:
        each flake traces cold pathways,
        arriving as gentle anarchists,
            upending the order of autumn's decay.
Garage doors wear white caps lightly,
    lines on clothes flutter with new weight.

How starlings scatter at the clap of boots,
        each a punctuation in the gray morning:
the trees hold their breath,
        heavy with a hush that is almost a presence.
    Nature performs its impartial soliloquy,
whispering life into the frost's sharp embrace.

    Here, seeds lie dormant, waiting
        for the thaw that speaks of renewal.
Below ice, the fierce clutch of earth
anchors both the living and the decomposed.
In these cycles, we find the footnotes of existence,
    inked in the silence of a snow-capped landscape.

Echoes of the Mundane

Through the cracked lens of everyday:
the way light shifts, subtle, across
   a can of beans—boneless ham rings:
in a dance of fluorescence, mundane
yet somehow fractally intricate;
each ripple a testament to time.

Seasons cycle in the pulse of produce,
    strawberry preserves gleaming like
captured sunsets in glass jars—
a mother, stooping, grasps for youth,
her list fluttering: save a life or find
a misplaced leash in isle five.

   Corners fold where notices cling,
fragmented appeals: return my dog,
lost amidst the echoes of aisle ends;
   where ads and life blur, tear-streaked,
echoing up yr nose with a soft surrender
   to the chaos that binds us, unseen.

Threshold Echoes

    The ding echoes: a mundane bell strikes,
   renewing the still air: life flutters—
    a chest lands, wood grained like aged oaks,
secrets nestled within like acorns
   awaiting the right soil: a season turns
in the hinge of a day—

Leaves whisper as if to divulge
  the ratios of sunlight and shadow:
how each leaf weaves through photons,
a dance of decay and growth,
roots sprawling beneath visibility,
threading through earth's dark manuscripts—

At the threshold, rationale meets instinct:
a sudden gust, the door swings wide,
    reveals the intricate veins of wood,
   its scent of ancient forests, recalling
the unopened, the stored-away:
     how tightly shut lips can speak volumes.

Subtracting Daylight

in mid-December's grip, cold sharpens:
    edges blur, the daylight thins,
a slow subtraction from morning
    and evening: the Mediterranean
heaves under the weight of her sorrow,
tainted waters, her gown of azure spoiled.

ground crickets sing beneath the frost,
    hymns to survival: their chirps,
        small sparks in the creeping dusk.
We gather, our breaths visible,
around fires, crafting light festivals,
    celebrating the retreating shadow.

    Yet, the air tightens, a reminder:
our choices echo, egg cartons
    and plastic—small gods of decay.
The cricket's song—a plea for resilience,
for wisdom to revere what is underfoot,
in the hope that our tithes might nurture rebirth.

Temporal Mingle

    Through the market's clamor, echoes bounce:
voices, colors swirl, contracts of life
that bargain with each passing second,
where old meets young in hurried exchange:
here, the busy stretch their youthful stride,
there, slow steps betray the weight of years.

Into the mist-shrouded valley, quiet:
    footfalls soften under vapor's cloak,
the sun a dim navigator, lost
in the folds of ceaseless grey, guiding
none but the wandering thoughts of those
pausing to hear silence speak in chills.

Beneath the skirts of shifting vapor,
    truth or illusion? Sun and moon trade
shifts: clarity fades, obscurity reigns.
No tirement like retirement: still,
paths weave through decay towards renewal,
each step a question, each breath an answer.

Choreographic Courses

Light dances through the leaves:
each leaf a note in the wind's score,
shadows sweep the understory—
    black notes flung down in a silent roar.
Sunlight threads through the high canopies,
forming rhythms of bright and obscure.

   Leaves rustle: a tremolo in the breeze,
branches sway: strings pulled by unseen forces,
the woods breathe a symphony, complex—
composed of infinite, transient sources.
    Each photon casts its fleeting text,
life and light entwined in choreographic courses.

Bark's rough script tells of years passed,
roots delve deep where dark soils thrum,
a crescendo of life where shadows cast,
every creature, every plant finds its hum.
In this orchestra of existence so vast,
    nature's notes resound, then succumb.

Temporal Contours

   Beneath the mist's soft shroud, lights blink:
a distant Christmas tree stands lone,
its twinkles cast on the silent lake,
ribbons of highway curling out—roads
     that thread from now to the infinite.
 The moon, a bright disc in the black sky,

hangs like a promise in the cold,
its pale light washing the world below.
Tree, celestial in lone virtuosity,
draws eyes, painting dreams on night canvas:
a scene set deep within the universe,
      where time pauses, heavy with wonder.

   The ephemeral glow shifts, transforms,
as mist slides over moonlit whispers.
Contours of reality blend and bend,
a dance of existence and illusion:
how fleeting our place in this vast expanse,
     all bound by the temporal and the endless.

Frost's Script

    Snow folds over the elm's broad arms:
each leaf a testament to silence,
a shroud in white, unbroken
yet perpetually fracturing: split
by the weight of unseen crystals,
    a lattice of ice and pause.

Under the muted sky, the garage roof
    slants sharply—new angles on old shelters:
where the stored tools rest, unstirring,
encased in the cold's embrace: steel
grows brittle, like the bones
    of the earth beneath frost's script.

Inside, the warmth tinkers with quietness,
while words simmer down to their essence,
stripped by the chill's sharp inquiry:
    language, a threadbare blanket.
It's the distance of stars unlooping,
where thoughts hover, unbound and raw.

Eternal Tangles

In the rush of hen pheasants: fleeting wings
snap against the low brush—nature's fleeting,
   yet, tangled in the eternal: roots cling
    deep where hidden streams whisper, repeating
  their ancient courses beneath the soil, cold
and dark, a permanence we walk over.

Yet, this ground, too, shifts—breaks—molds
itself anew: the chaotic order.
  Life's brief spark, contrasted sharply with
the enduring earth, cycles punctuated
   by each lively dart and earthly myth:
how we gauge the weight of years, unsated.

What do we know of lasts or firsts,
  in the thick of living: where invisibles
mix with the visible, a burst
of color against the gray, irreducible
complexity of being, the strands
of existence—so finely webbed, they tremble.

Thresholds of Dawn

In the half-light, dawn leaks silent hues:
    fragments of crimson, scattered on cloud's edge,
    tenuous as ice tendrils on winter glass:
nature sketches, lines drawn thin and urgent,
dissolving boundaries between night and morn,
the ephemeral ink of a world in flux.

Sun's first rays stumble through branches, tangled,
a web of shadows cast on frost-hard soil,
    each leaf a spectral lens, magnifying
the struggle for light, a delicate dance
of visibility, cloaked then revealed,
echoes of warmth creeping over cold ground.

    The horizon, a theorem posited
by the weary night: proving day must dawn,
where ice crystallizes into form like
    thoughts freezing into words on a blank page,
a landscape distilled to its raw essence,
briefly held before the thaw of true light.

Chiaroscuro Whispers

Under the ancient elm's broad reach,
shadows dance: chiaroscuro embroidery
on the green carpet — a play of dark
against light, simple yet profound.
    Leaves whisper: they know the secrets
of the sinewy, twisting light's tale.

Branches lace the sky, filigreed shadows
shift as a crow alights, and the world tips
into a new alignment: perspectives
are tossed like a breeze-scattered puzzle;
what was hidden in plain sight now stark,
revealed in the sudden flap and flutter.

The wind's breath stirs, an invisible hand
    that molds the scene, casts dapples
into a kaleidoscope of motion; below,
    our view shifts from earthbound roots
to an aerial tapestry of white, each limb
gently cradled in the soft embrace of snow.

Temporal Mimes

    Amid the whispers of the snow,
porcelain mimes glide, their faces aglow:
a mimicry of joy, thin as ice, fragile as silence,
    hiding the creases where laughter once echoed.
  Shadows under the hemlocks' bent boughs,
room for echoes of owls and hares,

their silhouettes a dance of persistence,
nature's puppetry, strings unseen.
Vinyl gleams beneath flickering neon,
sales tags flutter like leaves in gales:
this temple of the temporary, where old meets new,
    footsteps muffled by the promise of warmth.

The bay, swirled white and grey, captures:
whales cut through the ice, a cold so sharp
    it holds the breath of the world suspended,
    each fluke a cleaving of stillness,
snow drifting, heaping on the wind's slow step,
the sea moving, unburdened, forward.

Frost Whispers

Snowflakes descend like soft footfalls,
whispering secrets: they transform
   the elm, now a fortress in white, standing
     against the husky gray dawn; frost lines
       each twig, a circuitry of ice, delicate
and fierce in its cold design.

Through the window: a muted world,
   where the ordinary becomes enigmatic—
the low hum of a kettle, steam curling up
like spirits being released into chill:
here, in this room, the echo of a football
game spills over, yielding warmth.

   Sunlight fractures through icicle teeth,
a slow dance of light and shadows—
the paradox of warm glows against
   cold glass, pressing questions about
what stirs unseen beneath the snow—
nature's whispers, relentless, enduring.

Granite Whispers

In the whisper-thin veil of dusk,
light fractures on the mountain's brow:
here, where echoes bend and discuss
   the weight of unseen snow.
A cosmos captured in a glance—
each crevice holding night's advance.

The mountain, ancient, speaks in stones,
a language forged from earth's deep core.
Its silence cradling my bare bones,
   while shadows stretch and soar:
Small voices drift, caught in the chill,
yet hold a world in their soft will.

 Granite listens, unyielding, vast,
   to the fleeting dance of light and dark.
With each sunset, a history cast
      in lines quiet and stark.
A whisper, slight, against such might,
bears truth where day folds into night.

Seasons of Embrace

    Beneath thin veils of morn, the sky:
    a patchwork—blue against the gray—
        whispers of snow begin to lie
        softly, as if afraid to stay.
Trees hold the weight of transient grace,
etched sharp against the slow light's spread.

Uncle Archie's fresh earth face,
carved deep by years, now still, unread,
    lies beneath a blanket pure and crisp:
the final act of December's play.
His stories, folded in winter's lisp,
    echoes within the pines, they sway.

    Each flake, a verse of serene unrest,
mirrors our breaths in cold air cast.
With each gust, branches protest, yet
    bend, learning the art of holding fast.
    Seasons shift—embrace to release—
        while we clutch at ghosts, reluctant.

Domestic Orbits

Snow dusts the window's ledge, gathering:
    each flake, a whisper at the pane,
mingling with the steam of roasted meats.
    Aprons, stained with the day's toil, sway
gently: hung on hooks like tired sentinels
of domestic dances and secret recipes.

In these confined spaces, we orbit,
particles drawn in the gravity of home.
The wind, a deft sculptor of time and air,
  shapes the cloud's drift: a slow, sure brush
    across the canvas of a winter's day,
while pots simmer, mirroring the sky's gray.

  A thread of smoke rises, unbroken yet
thin as the veil between now and the unknown.
  Here, the festive table laid beneath
    these converging elements: a tableau
of laughter and clatter, seasoning
our shared existence, our transient warmth.

Winter's Murmur

    Snow muffles the garden's hardened crust:
the icicles weep as they lose their grip,
dripping testimony to cycles of thaw.
    Each droplet reflects a fraction of light,
bouncing, weaving through fibrous clouds,
transforming the mundane into prisms.

    Amidst this cold, a fragile peace prevails:
indoor blooms gaze out with tender envy,
   longing for the wild's harsh caress.
  Yew, stoic under its snowy shawl,
breathes softly as breezes sculpt
its edges, shaping resilience in shadows.

    As dusk descends, contrast sharpens—
delicate flora against the winter's might,
a subtle dance of survival unfolds.
Light retreats, pulling shadows tall,
    while nature whispers of endurance,
      a soft murmur in the silent, snowy eve.

Marsh Mithridatism

In the cradle of the high marsh, where sedge
leans into the fray, survives: woven strength
against the seep of poison, threads of life
    taut against the pull of human error.
Tiny flowers nod, the world's small applause,
   whispering resilience, fragile yet fierce.

  Under snow's deceptive purity, 'mons'
reveals reversed truths, hidden in plain sight,
   a landscape's mourning gown. Here, chemicals
lace through water veins, a silent creeping
that belies the marsh's serene façade.
The earth holds its breath, tiptoe on decay.

Yet, in the mire, lie glimpses of Mithridates—
tales of immunity, hope's stubborn pulse.
As nature scripts its loss in vanishing ink,
ripples linger on the water, echoes
of what was, or could have been, if not for
our touch: gentle, destructive, indelible.

Thaw's Dance

   Through woven branches, explorers press:
each step a story, rough and hewn,
   where leaves whisper of resistance,
the sky broad: a vast unclosed claim,
seducing them with its ceaseless expanse,
while roots clutch at their boots like past missteps.

The thicket parts: a sudden pond
breaks the surface: tension released,
revealing a flash of silver beneath—
a brief, bright journey caught in sunlight,
where ice might form, layer on slick layer,
mirroring the sky's cold, indifferent gaze.

   Yet, amidst this quiet freeze, a dance:
crystals form, intricate and sharp,
mapping out paths of subtle resistance,
   embedded deep where cold meets thaw.
The explorers, some pause, others push forth,
finding freedom in the crunch of snow underfoot.

Incremental Thaw

    Each day peels back a layer of chill:
the sun arcs higher, a slow brush
  of light unstitching the compacted snow,
and we, under this gradual warming,
    note the subtle shifts: a thaw in spirit,
buds tempting fate, green fragile tips.

    Awakened roots thread through softening soil,
  chemistry alive with whispers of growth—
    how molecules dance to the hymn of renewal.
Photons cast spells on dormant seeds,
and every inch gained in light,
  mirrors a stretch in our own perceptions.

  Critics draw lines, while poets blur them,
adding shades where light merges into shadow.
Isn't clarity itself a kind of mystery?
Reading the subtle, interpreting the bright,
    we find depth in the incremental,
understanding in the layers of light's return.

"Frost and Flame"

Morning breaks, clear glass defying frost,
its edges sharp as newsprint's sudden cut:
a bomb, LaGuardia, the broadcast crackles,
    disturbing the snow's serene descent,
where calm once played its silent notes
on wintry curtains, now pulled aside.

  I care not a fig, not for a fag in a fog,
as the old saying trips off a tangled tongue,
the stark difference between a flake and flame,
each falling, one burns, one blankets in cold:
such is the dance of days and disruption,
    threads intertwining, unexpected and sharp.

    Particles alight, the sky a chemistry set,
  precipitation mingles with human fears,
and yet, this windowed morning, so clear,
offers a pause: I watch, I weigh the view,
between the quiet chaos of nature's brush
and the loud intrusions of us, mere passersby.

Bridge of Whispers

Beneath the skull, hollow yet profound:
its caverns echo age-old wisdom cries,
a beacon through time's relentless tide,
casting light where shadows stretch too long;
yet, intact amidst our ruin and wrath,
    the skull, spared—the beacon in our night.

Neighbors, silent shadows at my side,
bond unseen, felt in the quiet dusk;
   their presence a subtle, steady pulse,
like stars unseen by day but always there,
    bridging gaps without a word or glance,
deep-rooted as trees that mark their bounds.

A log, once barrier, now path across:
   necessity crafts from our obstructions,
   transforming the simple into vital links.
When earth whispers of our fragile lease,
will we heed its call, or forge ahead,
blind to the bridge until it falls away?

Cityscape Mornings

Dawn cracks: high rises slice the soft
blue belly of awakening sky,
each window glazed with golden thoughts
of those rising, stirring, questioning
    what dreams linger in sleep's soft arms:
their echoes in steam-swirled coffee.

Pigeons, wings thrumming like heartbeats,
swerve in swarms, graffiti sky with
    urgency: fleeting shadows cast
on the sidewalks below, where feet
tread past remnants of moonlight, worn
as old coins in a beggar's cup.

Here, the constant hum—Neon buzz
and laughter clipped as a metro's turn.
  Each face brushes another, unseen,
yet each leaves a smear of soul: a brush
    of loneliness on crowded streets:
    we, moving, alone together.

Echo's Symphony

The rusted cart, wheels upturned:
a relic of haste, now stilled by time,
bog's embrace: a slow, sure burial.
Glass fragments scatter light, mirroring
   the fractured sky: each shard
   a story paused, half-told.

Mockingbird trills, the echo's tail:
mimicry of gone days, of engines,
sirens—now but whispers in the wind.
This chorus against the hush of heath,
    where sphagnum holds the dew like grief,
and stones mark the passage unobserved.

Here, the land speaks in sighs,
   brushstrokes of decay blend the old with new,
where nature cloaks old ambitions.
   In every rustle, a whisper of cycles,
the interplay of leaf, twig, and echo,
    each call a note in the symphony of survival.

Temporal Mirroring

The lake, a glassy stretch: calm and still,
reflects cedar tips, upright, pointing to
a sky bluing at the edges of day,
and beneath, fish teem—silver dashes
in water, cold molecules meshing
with warmer currents: transitions.

A temple stands, homage in stone,
built where nature's pulse beats loudly:
roots intertwine with carved foundations,
birdsong melds with echoes of chants—
a prayer in each leaf flutter,
    wind's whisper through the ancient halls.

Clouds gather, a brooding contrast
to the fire that sunset kindles;
light flares, then shadows deepen—
storm brews, as if the sky resents
    its peaceful portrayal in the lake's mirror,
morning waits—radiant, inevitable.

Internal Marketplace

Through the soft fold of the esophagus,
a slide greased with commerce: its slick walls
echo with the chant: save, save, save!
   Here, the descent spins into deeper zones,
each turn a booth for trade in the lit cavern
of my gut: this internal marketplace.

Down corridors of pulsing pink, where
   houseflies buzz, drift—ghosts of deals
      dead or dying—the blood's currency.
A twist, a bend, a dive deeper still,
into the cavernous intestines: endless aisles
stocked with promises, bright and consuming.

Skeletal shelves lay beneath tissue tarps,
each microbe tagged for quick sale.
The rumble of digested irony: what fills
must also empty, lost in the noise
of perpetual motion, the buzz,
the ceaseless barter of being.

Scatter of Resilience

    Grains scatter over crisp snow: each flake,
        a tiny mirror, reflects a stark sun,
neighbor's hands, coarse, woven through with veins,
        drop seeds that the cold earth will not claim,
but the pheasants will, their bodies heavy
against the wind, dance around frosted spruce.

Their tails, like fanfare in the silent freeze,
  swish, painting arcs of resilience in chill air:
here, life insists, pulses beneath feather
     and bark, where shadows deepen, yet suggest
light persists, gathering in the spaces
unseen, where roots and frozen soil commune.

Amid these cycles, such labor: mundane,
yet vital as the heart's hidden rhythms,
and the neighbor, pausing, breath a visible
cloud, sees in the scatter a kind of sowing:
hope casts wide as day ebbs, night's quiet
  ushering stars that navigate the dark.

Temporal Echoes

Mountains cast shadows over fleeting time:
    each boulder a silent testament to slow
    change, while rivers rush to shape the earth,
carving deep scars that will speak of mighty
force long after our echoes fade into
the silence of age-old stone.

  The cascade throbs with the pulse of millennia,
     high cliffs bearing witness: here stands permanence,
  here the rush of water, a vein cutting
    through the heart of terrain, relentless as
history, that writes its own narrative
without need for our fleeting scripts.

  Great peaks endure, underpinning the sky,
    roots entwined deep with the bedrock of ages;
  while we, transient, scrawl temporary lines,
so convinced of our stories' magnitude
until nature's vast breath whispers:
    listen, learn, and be humbly amazed.

Mechanics of Indifference

   Leaf shadows flicker, mechanics whirl:
     as gears of daily lives mesh, quietly
beneath the vast, indifferent sky.
The saw cuts through oak: firm, decisive,
mirroring the chop of relentless time,
grain upon grain, shaping echoes.

The wind gusts, a swift current of change,
sweeping sawdust, stirring cold ashes
from yesterday's long extinguished fires.
Hands, weathered like the wood they work,
align planks, patterns unseen but felt,
     nature's blueprint within human designs.

A sigh, the day wanes, tools rest:
    the bench stands, sturdy, unfinished,
   a testament to toil and tomorrow.
Stars blink on as the workshop dims,
in the quiet, the universe expands -
night's cool breath whispers of cycles unending.

Whispers of Growth

In the quiet growth of toenails, life whispers:
the slow tick of bone, keratin hardening,
shadows cast by the sun in shards of light,
each ray a story distilled in the spectrum:
here, the mundane breathes its importance,
nestled deep where roots drink silently.

Teeth, like white stones in a dark riverbed,
reflect the moon's pull on hidden currents:
    speak now of the force that shapes us, unseen,
and the decay that marks our passage through:
    all is movement, even in stillness,
the constant hum of cells in their dance.

The poet, like an old tree, absorbs the day,
truths laid bare by the angle of light:
while minds orbit thoughts like celestial bodies,
in the vast space between presence and absence,
we find the heart's quiet beating:
a pulse that echoes in the chambers of cosmos.

Winter's Mind

   Beneath the watchful pines, steps crunch:
snow compresses, a quiet symphony,
each flake: a note in the cold air's clutch,
   patterns known only to the drifting breeze.
Light filters through, a slow, golden rush,
   murmurs of warmth in the stark freeze.

Solitude walks here, a soft-spoken guest,
echoes of footfalls in wide, white halls,
the sky a vast sheet of stillness, dressed
   in hues that whisper of old, silent calls.
Snowflakes swirl, a dance unrepressed,
choreography writ on the wind's walls.

In this landscape, thought finds its pure form,
ideas crystallize like ice on boughs pine,
a mind reshapes in the storm:
tranquil, poised between line and line.
Yet, from frozen quiet, insights are born,
threaded through the soul, thin and fine.

Winter's Palimpsest

Snow falls: each flake, a soft sigh:
    a quiet curator of landscapes,
reshaping hills with whispers,
their voices hushed but potent
    as they blanket every landmark,
  silencing the seen world.

Through the wintry veil, voices fade:
echoes buried beneath white layers,
which sculpture new scenes, silently,
from the hand of December's chill:
    creating, while erasing traces,
of the world we thought we knew.

Underneath, the earth holds tight
    to seeds waiting for their spring,
  like thoughts paused in a poet's mind,
unwritten by the snow's erasure.
Yet, in this quiet, a promontory rises,
    built from layers of transformative cold.

Thawing Transactions

Each thaw drips time: a slow tick,
the land speaks in trickles and groans;
frozen intents, now warming to trick:
the toe heals, a market's tone shifts,
hope simmers in these small exchanges,
where balance teeters on the edge of spring.

Ice cracks, a lattice losing grip,
echoing traders' futile squabbles,
disappointments thaw, puddle beneath feet;
still, beneath, seeds of change gestate,
tiny victories in despair's retreat,
a quiet bloom in the chill's decrease.

Streams, newly bold, carve paths unseen,
as thoughts form tributaries, rushing:
is the trade lost or simply transformed?
    Landscape learns its strength in melt,
each drip a whisper of potential's rise,
nature's patient lesson: to endure and flow.

Chill Sublime

The frost heaves up in jagged spikes:
between the spruce, a pheasant darts,
scattering old snow with its flight,
    search for seeds in the cold twilight,
  while nature scripts its silent parts
in the crisp, encroaching dark.

Old lessons learned in warm confines
shiver, unsheltered, in these climes:
    knowledge freezes beneath new snow,
  lines blurred where once clear paths would show,
every step stirs the chill sublime—
a quiet breath in frozen time.

In the merging of path and plight,
the stark wild grasps the edge of night;
here, existence wears thin, reveals
  its icy core—the stark, the real—
under stark cedars, stoic, bright,
  our eyes adjust to fading light.

Winter's Dialogue

    Beneath the quietus of snow, land holds:
layers whisper of the night's cold grace,
a blanket woven finely, thread by thread:
each flake, a pause in the haste of time.
    Dawn breaks, each ray a sharp query
into the dark's soft, lingering embrace.

Heat murmurs to frost: yield, transform,
while light casts steel upon the white scroll,
scripting tales of thaw and renewal.
Silence, once deep, now trembles thin,
breath of trees exhaling, waiting,
       hoarfrost into dew, ice into stream.

Glimmer on a bough, the sun's discourse:
dialogue of warmth with the chill of dawn.
Shadows pull back, as if shy of day,
edges of ice retreat, water's slow applause,
each droplet reflects a fleeting world,
caught between ephemera and eternity.

Winter's Ballet

Beneath the gray vault of a February sky,
    the sparrow twitches: jittery script of bones,
syringe-beaked, threading through thin branches
    that sway not with wind but the pulse of fear:
a hawk circles above, as cold as the air
between the lifting of wings and the fall.

    This dance, nature's grim ballet, unfolds
where emotions raw as cut reeds bleed
    into the frost-hard soil: here rage, here love,
tangling in the undergrowth, unseen yet keenly
felt, like ice forming in the heart's hidden crevice,
unseen yet potent as the hawk's shadowed swoop.

Each gust transcribes grief across the marsh,
anger rustling the reeds, while somewhere beneath,
soft as the settling of snow on cedars, peace stirs,
   hope furtive, almost ungrasped, like a rumor
of warmth under winter's unyielding crust,
a promise held in the silent drift of seasons.

Erosion's Tongue

Lines warp and weave through moss-slung stones,
    each syllable a separate note of the landscape's song;
here, where the ground shifts beneath questioning feet,
    truth and illusion: twin serpents, swirling in a dance.
Branches curl like the tongues of liars, speaking
    in rustles, their whispers thin veils against the wind;

every leaf a compromise between revealing and concealing,
roots entangled in a relentless pursuit of depth.
The sky, too, tells tales in the palette of dawn and dusk,
her colors bleeding hues of honesty interspersed with deceit:
a canvas stretched at the edge of our perception,
beckoning, yet never fully yielding its secrets.

In this valley, the brook stutters over pebbles,
reluctant yet compelled to voice its path;
it murmurs of beginnings and, in the same breath,
of endings, weaving through the insistent pull of currents.
    Erosion—the land's slow speech, etching deeper meanings
into the silence, where time pools, gathers, and spills forward.

Thaw's Alchemy

In the slowly melting rim of snow,
the backyard's breath whispers of spring:
a pheasant pecks, where ice crystals glow,
   among hemlocks standing, unwavering kings.
     Below, the thaw's subtle alchemy unfolds
as winter yields to the push of green,

where once the land in frost was held.
Now, vibrant hints of life convene.
Beneath the hemlock's ageless guard,
bees hum to the rhythm of the new,
each buzz a small yet resolute charge
   against the still, the cold, the hue.

Their dance creates a warmth not felt by wind,
   which stirs no leaf nor bends a bough
in this place where seasons blend and mend.
Here, nature speaks: we only watch its vow.
     A pheasant's vibrant plume juxtaposes
the white retreat, a silent witness.

Seasonal Cadence

    Shadows weave through twilight's weave,
edges of light bend around old oaks:
    a storm broods, yet warmth breathes
from the thawing heart of winter's snow,
as if the earth, too, pulses with deep veins
of unseen rivers, lively and undimmed.

    Leaves rustle with the whispers of youth,
where an infant clenches hope in tender fists;
an ancient's eyes reflect the same skies
but rest now where shadows merge with soil—
Bach resounds, threading through the crisp air,
  melding now's urgency with eternity's pause.

    Notes climb, cascade in delicate fury,
    framing dawn's grey in bursts of clarity;
each melody a sharp reminder: life cycles,
seasons turn from frost to bloom, from birth
to the quiet dignity of closure, overlooked,
yet as certain as night's surrender to day.

Seasonal Constructs

Ditch water stirs, wakens from ice:
   spring pulses urge mud through cracks,
   thaw's whisper to dormant seeds.
Can you hear how winter bleeds
into spring, a slow dissolve
     of former selves, frost's firm resolve?

The thermometer, a fickle friend,
     sways: here at forty-five, where ends
begin, and youth's sharp green turns gold.
Tiny caterpillars, bold,
   inhabit leaves, munch through the day:
are they not, too, in decay?

Lines not drawn but felt, where wild
meets the manicured, child
of nature pressed against the glass
   of my own aging. Seasons pass,
yet I gaze, reflect: all flux
is mirrored in the soul's constructs.

Thaw's Philosophy

In the dim grasp of dawn, the snow clings:
thinly spread, like whispers on the land,
speaking in cold snaps and frosty breaths;
each flake, recalled by warmth, slips away—
   melting into the verses of spring's voice,
as flurries promise, falter, and fade.

   The bark feels the bite of the chill;
  it stands, a stoic observer, split
 between earth's pull and the lofty ideal,
where limbs wrestle with the weight of air,
grasping at sky, yet rooted in grit,
  a symbol stretched between seen and unseen.

Grass blades pierce the old snow's shroud,
  emerging green against the white's retreat,
resilient sprouts cheer the cycles:
decay folds into birth, endlessly,
underneath, all connected by a thread—
breathing, pulsing, woven by time's hand.

Whispers of Shape

In the hush of dawn, snow sifts: silence
layers onto the expanse of a frozen lake
where edges blur—tree to sky, land to echo,
    each flake, a wisp of chilled breath, collects
gently veiling the stark forms of winter:
the world softens, surrendering sharp edges.

The geese cut a soundscape, stark, slicing
    through the calm, their calls piercing the air,
      migratory paths marked high over frosted fields,
   lines drawn in the void, looping the tangible
     with trails of intent: here is motion, there, stillness,
a juxtaposition weaving through quiet drifts.

   Visibility shifts, gauze over eyes and breath,
   snow binding light, reflecting particles,
  scenes once vivid now whispers of shape:
a barn's roof, a forgotten fence line,
the profound outlines of life disguised,
      each surface cloaked in transformative calm.

Horizon Echoes

In the dimming light, camels cast shadows:
long, stretching towards the horizon where
  twilight plays with the edge of the earth,
blurring lines that were never truly drawn;
their humps, ancient hills moving silently
across the sandscape of ceaseless time.

The river murmurs stories: old as the
crumbling banks, a soft clash of water
against stubborn stone: always yielding,
always pressing, in a dance of resistance,
echoing the resilience of tiger lilies
that pierce frozen ground with verdant spears.

Sky shifts from azure to indigo, capturing
fleeting whispers of Babylon's mighty echo,
as day folds into the velvet of night and
memories weave through the threads of the now;
roots and shoots entwined, pulling together
towards a horizon that blurs into dawn.

Misty Interlude

Morning breaks gray: a canvas of fog,
veiling desires that stir too deep,
where shadows whisper of sunlight:
    perhaps today, perhaps not yet—
this push and pull of seeing and blind,
the heart's quiet ticking toward hope.

The weight of air, thick with unspent dreams,
    maps roads not taken, not seen:
each breath a stepping stone to the unknown,
the pulse of waiting: thick, charged—
    an electric dance with the unseen,
nature's soft lament in the mist.

    In this hour, fleeting as a half-caught thought,
life's brevity touches the soul's edge:
taut between the now and the never,
a tapestry woven with threads of maybe,
each twist a tale of could-be:
the sweet ache of almost in the air.

Season's Thaw

    Winter tightens: each twig sheaths in ice,
    crunch of step in crusted snow speaks—
silence deepened by its own echo:
   world, wrapped in shroud, pauses, reeks
    of stillness: tribulation's wreaths
cling, coldly woven, to the quiet land.

    Yet, beneath: life whispers in wait and
    seeds in the chill—worthy contradiction—
    promise sprouts not seen but sensed.
Gate of season slowly swings on its hinge;
ice-sheathed boughs, under sun's slow gaze,
yield, dripping resilience in each drop.

Car doors sealed, the windows blind,
yet light finds way, brilliant, brash:
glimmers through, unveiling hidden hues—
   slow thaw shapes shadows on the glass.
Persistence in such freeze: nature's breath,
    draws warmth from cold, blooms forth anew.

Thresholds of Unrest

Beneath the night's full weight, clouds burgeon:
   heavy, gravid with retained heat;
the world waits, breath caught in the grip
of its own turning, sensation of pending shift;
winds gather, specters at the curtain's edge ready
   to tear through the veil of stillness.

This force, cleaner of season's debris,
it sweeps—nature's broom—across
the clutter of last year's leaves, restless,
    unsettled by the same urgency found
in the human heart: always building or breaking,
    always in the throes of creation or decay.

Each branch, pushed into its place,
finds alignment within the chaos of movement;
a ballet of limbs, dancing to the tune
of pressure and release, repeating rhythms
     that teach us the beauty of order restored
after the wild disarray has passed.

Temporal Whispers

Morning rends the blue with gray:
   sudden breaks, where light filters through—
voices of the wind, harsh,
   whispered secrets of ancient fear,
mapping a sky fraught with change:
shadows cast by the fleeting clouds.

Each shape a diary of ages past:
   in the dance of swells and dips,
childhood's face peers out, then old age—
hands stretched, catching moments;
they slip through like water,
granules sanding the edges of time.

What stands firm as seasons flux?
   Mountains erode, rivers wander:
paths crossed, redirected by force
   unknown, unseen, as we walk—
footprints fill with rain, disappear,
   yet we step, seek, in the dance of days.

Transient Thaws

   Morning breaks: frost whispers on sidewalks,
the delicate sheet of yesterday's warmth gone:
tires hum, a relentless churn over crisp ice—
     here, we mark time, the ever-thudding pulse
      of season's shift: transient, like breath on glass;
tulips press up, signaling under snow's crust.

Echoed in the crunch: a dialogue between
   the decay of old roots and new buds poised—
hollyhocks buckle, weary, beneath the white,
   yet life stirs below, indomitable, insisting.
     Human voices blend: talk of meals, the mundane
     meets the metaphysical over morning coffee.

A basketball hoop leans, unfinished, against
     a backdrop of bristled pines, and the sky
    paints itself the pastel hue of hope reborn:
   gardens and games, the structures we build,
mingled with the chaos of nature's own brushpile—
in every corner, resilience: the clutter of existence.

Existence Erased

The elm whispers through leaves:
its robust trunk a spire in the sky,
yet beneath, roots fear the creeping rot—
Dutch disease, rings closing tight: oblivion.
Light filters through branches, casting
shadows of past summers, fleeting.

   Scarred bark holds the memory of storms,
etched by wind, yet still it stands:
a monument to resilience, to the tenacity
of life where death shadows each twist.
Yet, in this fight, a quietude speaks—
    language, our vessel beyond the void.

Each leaf a syllable, green against the blue,
falling, they script decay and renewal alike.
   Words twirl in the air, caught in a dance
of existence and erasure, where meaning
molds the void, fills emptiness with echoes.
here, amidst the silent testament of growth.

Thresholds of Thought

Whispers tread lightly on the page's edge:
each word, a hesitant step toward form,
uncertain as droplets on a spider's web,
caught between the urge to drop and the
    compulsion to cling, to create: connecting
narratives like stars stitched across the night.

Here, in the throes of the cosmos,
words swirl, ephemeral as mayflies in gusts,
    each syllable a spark caught before it fades,
struggling against the wind's erasure:
the mind, a linesman, strict, yet unsure,
  charts a path through chaos, seeking clarity.

Form emerges, retracts, like waves on a shore,
lines drawn and redrawn in the sands of thought,
    each iteration a closer reach towards the whole,
a tentative ballet of advance and retreat,
where meanings mutate, then settle momentarily,
under the gaze of an ever-watchful creation.

Seasonal Scrolls

Peas tumble from pods, green, fresh,
each one a tiny heartbeat against the hand,
beneath skies that shift: grey, then blue.
The wind whistles through the begonias,
asks them to dance: they bow, comply.
Their petals, water-heavy: a burden to carry,

yet they persist through the chill, the thaw,
seasons unroll like scrolls, history written
    in ice, then water, as icicles weep the past.
   How quickly sunlight turns the sharp to drip.
    A porch view shifts: from white-blind panes
to clearness, where each drop reflects

   a slice of warming world. Such contrasts!
    Time's craft—subtle, relentless: we watch,
 but miss the grandeur in the humble routine.
  Here, in the simplicity of shelling peas,
the universe pens its relentless saga,
ignoring our small acts, our brief scenes.

Season's Echo

Through the lens of a lingering frost,
    dappled sunlight breaks over ice:
      each droplet a tiny echo
of seasons' tender flux, their vying
      for a footstep that melts, holding
the earth in a warm embrace.

Shadows retreat as light rehearses
    its daily sweep: the rhythm, a soft
reminder of renewal prancing nearby.
A robin, flush with vivid red,
    darts through the stark whiteness—
a brushstroke of life painted swiftly.

Beneath, the seeds stir—sensing
their moment near, driven by an innate
    push towards birth: the pulse of spring
      whispering secrets only they hear.
Forgetting winter's harsh whisper,
they reach for that first kiss of light.

Frost Schemes

Morning breaks: the frost whispers its scheme,
curling under leaves not yet fallen:
    air, once warm, submits to the sudden cold,
a descent so swift, it leaves breaths hanging
visible, suspended, a slow dance of ghosts:
change, the only constant, reveals itself.

Each flake spirals in a delicate descent,
too fine for snowing, yet they tangle the air
    with threads of the inevitable freeze:
so do our plans unfold, in unexpected
flurries, the ground shifting beneath us:
    we stand, moments captured in icy frames.

Sunlight teases through clouds, a coy presence,
promising warmth but delivering none:
like thoughts of spring midwinter, sweet yet unreal,
the landscape holds echoes of yesterday's heat,
each blade of grass a brittle memory:
thus we navigate this life, changing, changed.

Interplay of Warmth and Whims

Morning cracks: frost whispers to the stream,
   its icy fingers softening at the sun's
tease: warmth that sneaks in, between
   gusts that bite, playful yet piercing,
trees shiver, shedding their icy casings,
birds chirp, unfazed: jays, sparrows in dance.

   Between them, life spins, a sudden spar:
husband and wife toss words like leaves
in wind: sharp, swirling with undercurrents
of love and annoyance, a strange harmony
   echoing the nature's fickle heart;
and they laugh, the absurdity clear.

   Skyward, cardinals flare against the gray,
daring the chill, their red wings clashing
with the softened blue, painting hope
   in flight: as they weave through air,
so do we navigate our whims, our woes,
a testament to enduring, to living beneath the vast.

Twilight Sculptures

Beneath the evening's languid sigh,
  the elm reaches up: limbs brush a soft,
unfurling sky: twilight sculpts light
across the leaves, whispers dive and dart
    through the coarse laughter spilling over
from the porch's edge.

A beadblack bug dances, red-eyed wings
fluttering with the intimate knowledge
of the air's curve: unseen, yet pervasive
as the spit we spin into words, vulgar
or cleansed, shaping our breath's invisible
sculpture, binding us tight.

  What's the measure of beauty in these
    small acts, the silent pulse in the growth
    of roots, in the tear of fabric from frequent
use? Here, the wild weaves seamlessly
with the worn chatter of day's end,
each holding the other, seen and seeing.

Thaw's Murmur

Winter's grip loosens: frost shatters,
ground heaves: breaths of soil and ice,
   roots twist, misshapen in the thaw's murmur;
  bark splits, harsh against the burgeoning silence,
wind claws through branches: a harsh whisper,
trees, skeletal: dance of the desperate.

Harsh gales yield to sighs: spring's prelude,
the mockingbird returns, voice slicing
through the last chills, a testament of survival;
rain, soft as whispers, kisses the raw earth,
bud by bud, life asserts its tender insistence,
green sprouts pierce the brown blanket.

    Continuum of rebirth: cycles spiraling,
each leaf unfurls like a slow revelation,
sunlight pools in the crevices of old stones,
the air, once sharp with cold, now hums warm,
   in every bursting stem, nature's quiet resolve,
beneath it all, the steady pulse: time flowing.

Transient Skies

Clouds churn: a dance of blue and gray,
their bellies full, yet starved in sway.
    Sky curdles like clotted cream in spoon,
horizon a seamstress, stitching monsoon.
Forms roil, yogurt-thick, then thin to rain,
as if deciding what to hold, what drain.

    Popcorn kernels, the first snowfall,
clattering to earth: changes unroll—
white cascades meeting the wet,
melding, parting, a half-made thought
never settling, never still,
each droplet's touch a fleeting kiss

on leaves that soon forget the bliss.
Rain and snow, intermixed, relent,
never clinging long enough to dent.
Snowflakes: ephemeral crystals in flight,
each a breath, exhaled by the night.
    Life, too impermanent to grasp.

Ripple Narratives

Each vowel in the brook's murmur:
a narrative unspun: threads shimmering,
catching the sun's query, answerless:
how does light fracture into stories?
The brook knows: shifts, carves through stone,
its silken surface: a mirror for sky's parchment,

reflecting clouds' somber drift: their morph,
the slow dance of shape to shadow.
In its cool depths, notions sediment:
whispers not voiced, heavier than pebbles,
yet, in their silence, a fortress of meaning,
    holding back the rush of easier truths.

Each ripple, a soft pulse under the moon,
conveying more in glance than grasp—
the brook, a vein threading dark earth,
folding through shale, loosening roots,
its voice a hush of broken rings,
    each syllable vanishing, unheld.

Unscripted Gracing

In a room chilled to a theoretic calm,
air parcels shift, controlled, yet not quite tame:
walls hold, but cannot the wild weather dam.
Invisible divides: blades of grass, the same
force divides our planned paths from feral sprawl:
ice ages press down, patient and immense.

    Outside: the wind has no master, nor name:
plastic bags dance upwards, unrestrained laughs
in the face of fan-whirred, artificial air.
    Yet from the sterile, a thought breaks through seams,
like seeds in sidewalk cracks, defiant, green:
    a small, unscripted gracing of the real.

Here inside, wing-gates swing, secrets spill
over thresholds, uncontrolled variables
in our equations of living spaces.
Precision: a hope, not a guarantee,
as nature scripts in sprawling cursive lines
beyond our margins, charting unseen paths.

Temporal Stillness

The wax figures stand: a still parade of time,
unchanging faces gazing at the flux
where fire dances, daring wax to melt.
Drip by drip, history reshapes itself;
each droplet a brief chronicle,
frozen, then lost in pools of transient light.

    Morning whispers through the leaves,
words moist with dew and the weight of dawn,
    every tree a stoic poet whose bark
encodes the sagas of sap and season.
Birds, those fleeting minstrels, flit
from branch to branch, their songs sewing seams in the air.

What marvels lie in ordinary days,
as light slices through the canopy in slivers
of brilliant, unintended artistry:
life's grand, unscripted ballet
where leaves compost into future soil—
the cycle of decay and rebirth, endlessly inscribed.

Whispered Dusk

In the late hues of day, hawks curl skyward,
their shadows stretch long over the old barn:
such a thin veil between now and memory,
each beat a pulse in the chest of the horizon.
Seasons hinge on such delicate mechanisms,
the tilt and yaw of earth, a father's laughter.

Contrails score the cerulean expanse:
as if to stitch the fabric of the fleeting sky,
  each thread laced with the chill of coming night.
Below, the creak of stilts swaying gently,
    holding up our past: a house, a heartland, aged—
wood groaning under the weight of stories.

The dusk blossoms into soft oranges and pinks,
    reflecting times when fear was only play,
and we, mere silhouettes against the fading light.
A bird startles from the underbrush,
its flight a line drawn towards the inevitable:
    all things return, reconfigure, like whispered dusk.

Winter's Whispers

Morning blushes, cold seizes the dawn:
air crisp as a snapped twig beneath boots,
snowflakes meander down, a soft ballet
   on the breath of a waking world: new and gleaming,
each flake, a whisper of frozen lace,
softly gathers, a cloak over the green.

  By noon, the ballet sharpens into sleet:
each drop a shard of mirror, reflecting gray skies,
falling faster, the weather strikes hard,
   ice coats each blade of grass, congealing
     nature's pulse; the heartbeat slows,
the land, a glassy still under storm's siege.

Dusk brings a hush, snow to gritty dust,
     the day's colors leeched, leaving only shades
   of silence: the world, now subdued,
wrapped in the cold's tight shroud:
   this blanket mutes, tucks in the roots,
beneath, life whispers, waits for the thaw.

Winter's Symphony

Snowfall layers past layers: each flake,
a soft pulse in the vast, muted dome.
The silence is white: deafening: complete:
winter's own breath, slow and rhythmical:
    Fields furrow under crystalline weights,
the land bends, whispers in cold, creaking.

Snow-dancers pirouette on frozen lakes,
ice refracts, splinters light into prisms.
Trees stand robed in heaviness, branches
   bow like monks in silent prayer, laden:
     Through the white, a distant murmur—
perhaps the stir of a thaw, Beethoven's

   notes hanging, suspended in chilly air.
 The relentless march of snow, each flake:
   a composer crafting symphonies,
     swept across the expanse—silent, deep.
Continuous: the cycle of freeze, thaw,
    each breath of wind sculpts anew.

Entropy and Echo

The forceful sun: a truth ungentle, harsh,
each ray, a sentence declared on the dry earth,
the soil selves, parched, still cleaving to damp
   echoes of a rain: how memory survives:
beneath this stark illumination, life
whispers, withdrawing, into shallow brooks.

A brook runs—defiant against the day's
   glare, small braveries in liquid form;
traces of resilience etched on wet stones,
each droplet—a microcosm of struggle,
binding: the dance of atoms, mortal
yet ever renewing, a cycle aged in light.

Here, I witness: entropy and echo,
nature's fist clenches around what remains;
   the land does not yield easily to time,
nor does the human heart cease its own beat,
even as shadows lengthen, merging,
across the terrain, whispers become night.

Surface Depths

Eyes, not feet, climb: the spectrum calls,
    diving deep where the lake's mirror holds
stories in its unfathomed deeps: here
lies the paradox: seen surfaces and
     unseen depths, navigating both by sight,
with clouds beneath, sky grounded in reflection.

Spring's austerity stretches sprouts, thirsty,
anticipating the rain like a promise whispered
in the rustling, dormant, awaiting leaves.
Early tulips dare to bloom, petals catching
transient showers: a brief embrace of droplets,
    nature's flirt with time and timing, delicate.

Butterflies trace paths air writes, wings
    too light for burden, carrying only beauty –
    and the brook's song, indifferent to audience,
     flows on, a steady pulse beneath the chaos of daily
sunrise and set, marking nothing but the passage:
    each ripple, a muted whisper of staying, going.

Endless Cycle

A single figure winds through the quiet giants,
    each step a small note in an ancient hymn,
wind whispers: there is more within the less.
Amid the stoic peaks and valleys deep,
each brown stick: a testament to resilience,
green shoots sprouting: tiny bursts of defiance.

This landscape: vast, indifferent to breath,
    mountains, sentinels, inhale time,
exhale winter's cold, take in spring's warmth.
Scale: each leaf an epic unfolding,
the silent work of growing—slow, unseen,
yet carving the wind, the light, the earth,

as roots clutch earth, ceaseless in their pursuit.
In this resolute march of life and death,
a mountain's shadow dwarfs our transience,
still, every tiny blade of grass climbs toward light.
    Nature, the quiet observer, does not cease,
its breath a cycle of endless renewal.

Philosophy in Motion

  Beneath the canopy: two birds, one dance,
wings flutter against the quiet sky,
each beat a drum, soft yet distinct,
sounding through the tangled hemlock marches.
     Cardinal flashes red, a vivid sprawl,
against the willow's droop: nature murmurs,

      subtle are the shifts, the delicate balances
that tip seasons and life from one to the next.
Passerby pausing, eyeing the slow sway,
asks out loud, to no one or the wind,
"How swift does my own journey glide?"
     Separating leaf from limb,

the small bird, unseen in the dappled light,
is philosophy in motion, unassuming:
it alights on branches that hold answers
to questions not yet asked by us below,
each flutter dissecting our gathered years—
the conversation of flight and pause.

Fracture Symmetry

The room holds still: the urn, shattered,
edges sharp as splintered bone,
echoing the fractures of a deeper break:
how tradition spills, uncontainable,
    like sand through the notched waist
of an hourglass long unturned.

Silence hangs thick, each shard
a syllable in the long sentence of decay,
cutting the bare soles of those who tread
   too near the precipice of past and present:
     a balance, delicate as the surface tension
on a pond skimmed by skipping stones.

But within every break, a binding:
    flasherlaserlasher slashermasermasher,
 chaos cries in cracks, yet sings symmetry,
drawing eyes to juxtapose jagged lines
   with the slow, certain curve of dust settling,
     the room breathes—inhales the eternal.

Web of Unself

In the thicket's heart, where light dims:
threads of sunlight split by ancient limbs,
   each ray a story, filtered, faint,
yet strong enough to paint the quaint
mosaic of leaves and life: the thrum
of a world unsung, in green succumbs.

Byways where the marsh meets sky,
herons draft their arcs so high,
each wingbeat sculpts the humid breeze,
and in such breaths, I seize the ease
of nature's pulse: beat and flow,
  the lore we forgot, yet still, it grows.

    In the whisper of the big timber's call,
secrets of the earth are drawn:
roots tangled with tales of rise and rot,
identity not lost, but caught
in webs of bark and blade—transformed,
where self and unself are newly formed.

Convergent Divergence

Sunset burns: a vivid red fury
against the calm of vapor lines:
  intersections in the dying light
    where journeys cross, yet never merge.
The earth whispers its cool serenity
  into the chaos of my breath.

    The northern hermit thrush, discreet
with a song less fluid, still rings
with a clarity that pierces the tumult
of my raging heart: a liquid bell
in the silence of encroaching dusk,
    echoing through the fir and cedar.

As night descends, the world softens,
  rage diffuses into stars' faint glimmer,
each a distant sun, pulling the weight
of my small sorrows into the vastness.
Depression lifts as light recedes,
and peace bleeds into the dark canvas.

Echoes and Horizons

In this abandoned town, whispers slide:
like oil, slick, beneath the silent shades
of gas pumps, offering echoes cheap,
undrunk by any but the rusting sighs
of hinges that once articulated lives;
    the market's empty, shelves barer than bone.

Weatherman charts storms that no one sees,
his forecasts a litany of might and if:
overhead, clouds gather like dark thoughts,
a pressure drop foretelling storms not yet spilled
on asphalt empty of footprints and laughter;
futures, predicted but never unfolding.

The blackened edge of the horizon hints
at thunder, like a rumble of engines lost.
    Spruce worms weave through leafy manuscript,
each thread a subtle testament to cycles
of growth and decay in a world still spinning
despite the silence that thickens with dusk.

Breath of the Void

Through the hush of night: sharp, vast
  blackness unfolds, dense as thought,
  where stars, in sparse scatterings, hint
at order: light chinks in the heavy cloak,
    the universe expanding, breath by breath,
quarks trembling in the gravity of moments.

    Silhouettes of giant shrubs loom, threats
or guardians: interpretations vary by heart's
    beat: faster now, with the wolf's shadow,
      or slower, contemplating the cosmos' cold sweep,
contradictions cradle the core of being:
how darkness shapes the light we chase.

Fleetingness ties us—roots and wings churned
in the same soil, the same stir of sky:
each step in the night a brush with void,
yet also a touch of the infinite spiral;
loss dances with gain, empty hands grasp
fullness, the cycle sharp as starlight, endless.

Stone to Bone

The wall rises: rough, unyielding, cold,
   etched by the hands that faltered
   before mine: seeking the same ascent—
their struggles pressed into sediment,
layered stories binding: stone to bone.
Time's patient carving: water, wind,

whispers of the dog's ghost: unseen, unheard,
   below the roots where life insists, persists,
   and catkins are fierce lions, small yet bold:
each a universe, a fierce recluse.
I climb, my skin worn thin by rock,
the terror—my lion—gnaws, familiar.

    Such height! A vista of pain and promise,
   where very breaths forge new exoskeletons,
translating solitude to armor,
tough petals against the march of decay.
   In the shadow of each shell: the crawl,
     time's texture, weaving through fibers.

Cosmic Necessity

In the core's fire, the sun: bound, not boundless,
compelled to blaze, tracing circuits of necessity,
its flare lashing the dark void: a compulsion
to emit light and heat, like a breath
inevitable, sighed from cosmic lungs,
deep in the stellar forge of fusion.

Beneath the faucet's drip: a minute adjustment,
    a bucket aligned, catching life drop by drop;
here too, the urge, subtle but persistent,
to sustain the small, buzzing beings at play,
their dance around the pail a mirror
   to celestial orbits, gravity's soft tug.

Flowers tilt their faces skyward, not by choice—
driven by the same force that fuels the stars,
each petal, a testament to the push of life,
stem and stamen orchestrated by scripts
written in the code of cells, pulling and responding,
as earth and heaven loop in endless dialogue.

Frost's Retreat

   In a cold grasp, we rest:
each breath a cloud, each sigh a story
told in whispers to the frozen air:
  the beetles crawl where once a gaze held sway,
orbiting decay like planets, stoic,
cold to the cosmic dance of life, of death.

Snow mantles the rough cedar boughs,
draping the world in cruel, serene white
  while beneath, the ceaseless cycle turns:
flesh yields to soil, bones whisper to roots,
and all that lived succumbs to silence,
   muffled by winter's unyielding shroud.

Yet, spring hints in the thaw's subtle drip,
in the resilience of buried seed:
   time's pulse thrums beneath the frost's retreat,
revealing life's tenacity, its claim:
   nature marks us, we mark it in turn,
ephemeral scripts written on the wind.

White Whispers

Snow falls, not one flake like the other:
each a pattern suspended in chill,
   a hush descends as if the world softens
its breath under the weight of white whispers.
Movement stilled but not the mind's churn:
frost bites into thought, expanding the gaps.

Beneath this cold, stark canopy,
each flake floats down—gravity's soft mercy—
   touching earth, transforming the known
with a blanket, seamless and seclusive.
Contours of the familiar blur: where
     does one edge begin and another fade?

   In this white maze, all paths merge,
each step a silent dialogue with the abyss.
The room's warmth is deceptive: hearts
    race in tight orbits, thoughts freeze mid-air.
     Outside, the endless grace of falling snow
mirrors our fleeting stance against time.

Celestial Thread

   Times cascade like a river's rush:
   we stand, minute, under infinite arches,
each star a note in the cosmic hum,
   our years marked less in days
than in the slow dance of galaxies.
Spaces vast between each breath:

   We ponder the irony: our strength
found in vacuums, in vast emptiness,
mirroring the void where possibilities
unfold like the petals of night's bloom.
Here, a truck moves, relentless as time,
every turn a chapter in the novel of now:

Beside my bed, a simple plant breathes,
connected to celestial movements unseen,
   its life a quiet testament to the beauty
   of survival in both dirt and darkness.
As humans transition from earth to star,
we are bound by the same thread of existence.

Canvas of Truth

    Beneath the canvas of rinsed blue,
mountain peaks, chalk-dusted truth:
winds carve myths in cold white stone,
  whispers of the deep unknown.
Catkins fall, soft thuds on soil,
earthworms stir in transient toil.

    Dreams of skies cascade on high,
ponder the sea's sharp, saline sigh.
  The light strokes boughs with tender grace,
each leaf a story, time's embrace.
    Where we stand: spectators, scribes
writing the pulse that throbs, survives.

Through the lens of quivered light,
the universe unfolds—sheer, bright.
Existence: a query, vast, unspent,
  life's fabric, intricate and rent.
Vivid scenes dance, shift, parade:
our eyes, our souls, both deeply swayed.

Memory's Current

Light glitches the stream, where memories pool:
Father, your voice skims the water's edge,
tracing where soft moss and hard stone merge,
    echoes scattering like startled minnows.
  How can absence weigh so heavily
as the night's cold settles on my shoulders?

Each murmur of the brook a syllable,
lost to the vast, indifferent sea of time:
but here, in these whispers, I seek your face—
the reflection fractured by the current,
glimpses in the rush: are you still with me,
watching how the leaves gather in the flow?

    Oh, the decay of leaves to loam, and thoughts
to shadowed, unspoken dreams at twilight.
Each evening's dimming light a reminder,
    a closure ungrasped, a story unfinished,
  wherein the heart beats a rhythmic mourning,
hope rising with the fog over the marsh.

Edge Resolves

Steps echo shallow puddles:
a decision made in the drift
   of small waves, at the edge
of certainty and the damp sand,
   water seeping over cloth,
barely a whisper against skin.

Each step a minimal risk,
a quick breach in comfort—
the inevitability lays clear:
wet feet, a cold, clinging trace,
nature's soft applause in
     the lap of gentle currents.

There, where the water meets
the resolve, a subtle embrace:
tiny currents swirl, elements
converge in a simple, profound ritual,
a moment weighted by the ordinary,
each drop a testament to the journey.

Brooksong Essence

Water maps the land, bending:
   each turn shapes its song—
ripples catch light: interplay
     between sunbeam and shadow,
mirroring, a slow dance
of force and delicacy.

The brook murmurs undergrowth's
   liturgy, channels the pulse
of rain-soaked earth, swelling:
a vein throbs with runoff,
     its clarity a measure of speed,
its murk, depths stilled by storms.

Art strains to emulate this:
     fluidity scripted in serene strokes,
palette dipped in nature's hues,
the canvas—a silent brook
running deep, running true,
     sketching soul's subtle creases.

Endurance Paradox

Creaking limbs, stark: the dead trees stand,
etched against the sky's vast canvas—
their brittle forms a silent testament
    to what endures, and what fades away:
yet in each twig, the wind whispers tales
of seeds that sleep, awaiting spring's call.

Waters dance around stubborn roots,
softly shaping the unyielding:
such is the paradox of persistence—
hardness worn by the persistent flow,
the river scores its path, unseen yet deep,
a mirror to our own carving of place.

  In these shifts, a quiet stirring of the air:
leaves rustle, though no leaves are there—
    ghosts of seasons, spun through branches
as memory blends into the land's deep scars,
echoing the heartbeat of the soil,
where nothing lost escapes the whole.

Seasonal Self

In the silk of my mind, winds weave through:
frigid gusts meld with the tender bloom,
a cheek brushed by both flurries and dew,
where thoughts scatter, wide as the plume
of clouds that race in a tumult sky,
every shift a whisper: who am I?

   Leaves swirl in a dance of amber flame,
     each twirl a tale of summers past:
   the identity I cannot yet claim
quests through seasons that do not last.
In this chaos of fall and rise,
I seek the stillness beneath stormy skies.

Branches bear the weight of new snow; beneath,
roots clutch at the shifting, fertile earth.
Aurora crowns the night, a wraith
of light where dark and bright find birth.
   Here, where frosts and warmth collide,
I grasp my being before the tide.

Temporal Waltz

In the sullen haze of May, a day split:
mowing grass whispers to the morning,
shoveling echoes against the chill.
Each motion blends life with its fading,
a seamless waltz: decay and bloom.
By the ditch, hardly a scar on earth,

   dandelions rise in defiant bursts,
      yellow heads nodding to the rhythm
of a universe, indifferent yet cradling.
Slugs trail silver, stitching leaf to leaf:
a map of mundane, profound journeys.
Nature watches, unblinking, as time

weaves through thin veins of grass.
The man pauses, breath clouding above
     the quiet dichotomy of green and white,
pondering the resilience housed in frailty:
how life insists, persists through soft whispers
of dying things in cold embrace.

www.ingramcontent.com/pod-product-compliance
Lightning Source LLC
Chambersburg PA
CBHW011254040426
42453CB00016B/2427